Movement in Steady Beat

Other Movement and Music Materials by Phyllis S. Weikart

Books

Movement Plus Music: Activities for Children Ages 3 to 7, Second Edition

Movement Plus Rhymes, Songs, & Singing Games

Round the Circle: Key Experiences in Movement for Children

Teaching Movement & Dance: A Sequential Approach to Rhythmic Movement, Fourth Edition

85 Engaging Movement Activities, Learning on the Move, K–6 (with music CD)

Recordings

Rhythmically Moving 1–9

Guides to Rhythmically Moving 1–5

Available from
High/Scope® Press
600 North River Street, Ypsilanti, Michigan 48198-2898
ORDERS: phone (800) 40-PRESS, fax (800) 442-4FAX
Web site: www.highscope.org
E-mail: press@highscope.org

LEARNING ON THE MOVE
Ages 3-7

Movement in Steady Beat

Second Edition

Phyllis S. Weikart

HIGH/SCOPE® PRESS

Ypsilanti, Michigan

Published by
HIGH/SCOPE® PRESS

A division of the High/Scope® Educational Research Foundation
600 North River Street
Ypsilanti, Michigan 48198-2898
(734) 485-2000, FAX (734) 485-0704
press@highscope.org
www.highscope.org

High/Scope Press Editor: Lynn Taylor
Cover design, text design, and production: Margaret FitzGerald, Metaphor Marketing Inc.

Library of Congress Cataloging-in-Publication Data

Weikart, Phyllis S., 1931-
  Movement in steady beat : activities for children ages 3 to 7 /
Phyllis S. Weikart.-- 2nd ed.
      p. cm.
  ISBN 1-57379-130-X (Soft Cover : alk. paper)
 1. Movement education. 2. Games with music. 3. Rhyming games. I.
Title.
  GV452 .W435 2002
  372.8'68--dc21
                                2002151529

Printed in the United States of America
10 9 8 7 6 5 4 3 2 1

Contents

Action Songs 33

Preface

This expanded and revised book is now part of the *Learning on the Move* series, developed by the Movement and Music Education Division of High/Scope Educational Research Foundation, and is an activity supplement to *Round the Circle: Key Experiences in Movement for Young Children* (2nd Ed.) and *Teaching Movement & Dance: A Sequential Approach to Rhythmic Movement* (5th Ed.). It is one of several activity books in the series that are targeted at young learners (preschool and kindergarten). The other books published so far are *Movement Plus Rhymes, Songs, & Singing Games* (2nd Ed.), *Movement Plus Music: Activities for Children Aged 3 to 7* (2nd Ed.), and *85 Engaging Movement Activities*.

The rhymes and songs in this book will help children learn how to feel and maintain steady beat. These activities introduce children, ages 3–7, to a wide range of enjoyable and effective beat-keeping movement experiences.

The ability to feel and maintain steady beat is important for children to develop in early childhood because we believe children with this ability will be better able to master concepts in language and literacy, mathematics, and other content areas as well as increase their body coordination and related physical abilities.

This updated and revised book will be a useful addition to your movement and music materials for young children.

I would like to extend grateful appreciation to my family and persons in the Education Through Movement network who have been so supportive and helpful to me. I offer heartfelt thanks to my editor, Lynn Taylor, and to graphic designer Margaret FitzGerald of Metaphor Marketing for the production of this book. In addition, I extend a special thank-you to the creator of the musical scores, Lisa Jernigan, and to Karen Sawyers, Assistant Director of High/Scope's Movement and Music Education Division, who has been most helpful throughout the writing process.

Introduction

The *Education Through Movement: Building the Foundation* program
uses a **movement-based learning process** that is patterned after the active
learning preschool curriculum developed by the High/Scope Educational
Research Foundation (fully described in *Educating Young Children: Active
Learning Practices for Preschool and Child Care Programs,* (Second Edition).
In this program, children and teachers are *partners*—mutual initiators and
supporters of learning.

Later in this chapter we provide a brief overview of each of the four
components of this movement-based active learning process:

- **Key experiences in movement**
- **Movement core**
- **Teaching model**
- **Teaching strategies**

This is the delivery system that you will use to provide children with
exciting and worthwhile active learning experiences in movement.

How to Use This Book

The activities in this book are designed to supplement those found in
Round the Circle: Key Experiences in Movement for Young Children
(Second Edition). Please refer to that publication for a complete description

of the **movement-based active learning process and eight movement key experiences.** Also, *85 Engaging Movement Activities* contains suggestions for activities for kindergartners and elementary-aged children.

This book focuses on helping young children learn about the specific movement key experience **feeling and expressing steady beat,** although you will also be able to identify many other High/Scope key experiences (see sidebar, at right, for a list of the eight movement key experiences).

Youngsters who can feel and maintain steady beat will possess *basic timing*—a fundamental ability that should be mastered before a child enters elementary school. Developing this fundamental ability at an early age gives children a head start in at least three important areas of development: **motor skills, musical skills, and academic abilities.**

Movement Key Experiences

Moving in nonlocomotor ways (anchored movement: bending, twisting, rocking, swinging one's arms)

Moving in locomotor ways (nonanchored movement: running, jumping, hopping, skipping, marching, climbing)

Moving with objects

Expressing creativity in movement

Describing movement

Acting upon movement directions

Feeling and expressing steady beat

Moving in sequences to a common beat

The activities are divided into two major categories—**rhymes** and **action songs.** To help children organize steady beat movements for each rhyme or song, you can use the easy and effective *learner SAY & DO process.* The SAY & DO process, when used consistently, is very effective. Quite simply, SAY & DO means that children *say* the words that define their actions (SAY) and they *match the movement to the words* (DO). The synchronization that results from this experience helps children develop a cognitive-motor learning link and also helps them identify the steady beat inherent in a particular rhyme or song.

Organization of Rhymes and Action Songs

Each activity is divided into the following components:

Title: The title of the rhyme or song is provided, along with the melody's original title when applicable.

Text: The words or accented syllables to the rhyme or song are presented in **bold type** to identify rocking or patting motions or are <u>underlined</u> to identify the stepping beat.

Age: The range of ages for which the activity is generally appropriate.

Key experiences: A list of the major movement key experiences that the activity addresses is presented, including feeling and expressing steady beat.

Curriculum concepts: Generally, you will want to decide on one concept that most represents the reason you have chosen this activity (in addition, of course, to **feeling and expressing steady beat).**

Description of activity: A brief overview of the activity.

Materials: The equipment, if any, that is needed for an activity.

Activity to experience: The suggested lesson plan for initiating the activity. You may wish to add other steps or leave some out, depending on the age and experience of the children. Also, always encourage the children to engage in *active* explorations as they participate in an activity, to share their ideas with one another and with you, and to be leaders of the various activities. In most of the rhymes, an **anchor word** is provided to be recited four to eight times to the leader's beat to bring the group to synchronization before the rhyme is spoken. With songs, add an **anchor pitch** (first pitch of the song) to give the children the starting pitch. *Example:* Natasha is the leader. She begins to pat her knees in a steady movement. The teacher and other children join Natasha, matching her movement. The teacher says, "Beat, beat, beat, beat" (the anchor word) to synchronize the movements before saying the rhyme. Then the group sings a song ("Twinkle, Twinkle Little Star") and the process is repeated except that the teacher sings first pitch of the song (the anchor pitch).

Facilitation and reflection: Ways that you might extend children's thinking, with suggested questions to pose. The exact wording of the questions will be up to you. Notice that most of the questions do not have one correct answer. Wait awhile after you pose the question and encourage several children to offer their opinions.

Extensions: Additional ideas are presented for other ways to do the activity or to make it more appropriate for older or younger children. *(You can also use the extensions to do the activity in a different way at another time.)*

Musical Score

A musical score is provided for each of the action songs. A CD containing the rhymes and songs is included with this book. Use this CD to learn the rhymes and songs yourself so you can introduce and sing them with the children. We recommend that you do not play the CD in the classroom or center setting because the children need to hear *you* actually singing the songs. You could place the CD in the music area for children to use during work time to repeat activities they have enjoyed.

A Movement-Based Active Learning Process

As noted earlier, the movement-based active learning process described briefly here and fully in *Round the Circle,* consists of four major components:

- **Eight key experiences in movement**—The eight key experiences in movement for children aged 3–5 are listed on page 2. These experiences provide the framework for the movement-based active learning process. We use these key experiences to recognize, support, and extend the preschooler's fundamental abilities in movement. These important key experiences are among the **58 key experiences in child development** identified by High/Scope Educational Research Foundation as necessary for successful early learning. They affect many aspects of children's social, emotional, cognitive, and physical development.

- **The movement core**—The movement core, illustrated in the diagrams on page 5, is a summary of the motor development base for purposeful movement for all ages in the High/Scope *Education Through Movement —Building the Foundation* program. Aspects of the movement core have been modified to meet the needs of young children. Note that one of the movement core diagrams is labeled "nonlocomotor" and the other is labeled "locomotor." The text inside the circle of each diagram refers to the way the body can be organized for purposeful movement. For any age, "two sides" moving symmetrically is the easiest way to begin experiencing nonlocomotor movement (two fists pound), while "alternating sides" is the easiest way to begin experiencing locomotor movement (marching, tiptoeing). The movement complexity is illustrated in each diagram from top to bottom with the easiest movement at the top and the more complex at the bottom. As you introduce movement activities to young children, keep in mind this simple-to-more-complex way of moving. The words placed around the circle of each movement core diagram refer to the ways the body executes purposeful movement. A single movement (pat, shake) is easier to do than a sequenced movement (bend/straighten, or push/pull), and a static movement (one that pauses) is easier to do than a dynamic movement (one that keeps going, such as patting).

- **The teaching model**—The ease with which children, young people, or adults grasp movement activities or interpret directions often depends on the way the activities or directions are presented to them. This is why we offer you a **teaching model and movement core.** The teaching model can be used to engage children in all types of enjoyable movement-based activities. For children to experience success, you should be consistent in your approach and should be aware of the developmental levels of the children involved. The teaching model has three major components: **separate** (demonstrate *or* tell *or* use hands-on guidance), **simplify** (begin with what is easy or manageable to learn), and **facilitate** (engage children in using action, thought, and language). The sidebar on page 6 provides a handy summary of the teaching model.

Movement Core
Nonlocomotor

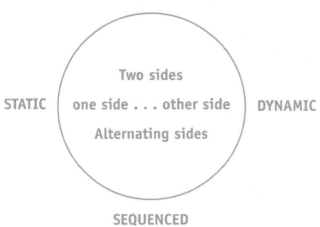

- **Teaching strategies—**

✔ Select activities at first that have a simple way of moving, such as patting against the body. All of the activities, except those that begin with a sequenced movement (bend/straighten) have a simple way of moving.

✔ Emphasize the steady beat by using an anchor word or anchor pitch that matches the movement. Do the movement first, say or sing the anchor word four to eight times to establish the steady beat, and then chant the rhyme or sing the song.

Movement Core
Locomotor

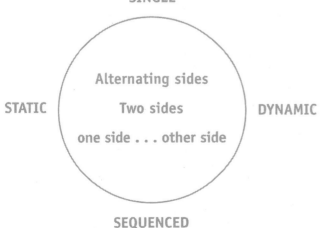

✔ At first, select the rhymes or songs you are most comfortable with and that enable children to remain in their personal space instead of moving about the room.

✔ When children are engaged in alternating foot movements, avoid saying "right" or "left" foot so children can begin with either foot.

Teaching model

Separate: Demonstrate or tell or use hands-on guidance.

Simplify: Begin with what is easy or manageable to learn.

Facilitate: Engage children through action, thought, and language.

✔ When a child leads an activity, match the child's movement with an anchor word.

✔ If the rhyme or song has more than one verse, pause between verses to reestablish the steady beat.

✔ Pitch the song high enough so children can sing. (Children's vocal chords are short, so they need a higher pitch.)

Rhymes

Curriculum
Concepts
Steady beat

Passing objects to others

Moving and speaking

Key Experiences
in Movement

Moving in nonlocomotor ways

Moving with objects

Feeling and expressing steady be

Ages 5-7

Aka Backa Soda Cracker

Children keep the steady beat while first listening to and then saying the rhyme and passing beanbags to one another.

Aka backa **so**da cracker,
Aka backa **boo**;
Aka backa **so**da cracker,
Pass to **you**.

Materials

Beanbags or soft balls

Activity to Experience

Children sit in a circle. They keep the steady beat in a place of their own choosing as they listen to you chant the rhyme several times. Children join in saying the rhyme as they become familiar with it.

Ask the children to hold their beanbags and to observe in which direction the beanbags will be passed at the end of the rhyme. Model, without speaking, a possible direction (right) for the children and have them identify the direction. The children then say, "Pass to you" and place their beanbags on the floor in front of the person on their right in the circle.

Once the children appear comfortable with both the rhyme and the movement of the beanbags, suggest that one of them begin keeping steady beat and then you can add the anchor word "beat" four times to bring all to synchronization before actually saying the rhyme. At the last line—"Pass to you"—all the children pick up their beanbags and pass them to the persons seated on the right. Repeat the game several times with various children being the leaders. Try passing to the left also.

Facilitation and Reflection

How did you know when to pass the beanbag?

Which way did you prefer to pass the beanbag? Why?

Extensions

Hold the beanbag in one hand and pass it to the lap of the next person on the word "pass."

Use sequences of movement, e.g., knees, shoulders, while saying the rhyme.

Instead of patting the steady beat, step or walk it. For the last line, substitute "Jump with you." The hop, gallop, and skip are other movements that could be used for identifying the steady beat.

Preschool children: Change the last line to "How are you?" or "I like you." Have your preschoolers make up the last line.

Curriculum
Concepts
Steady beat

Rhyming words

Awareness of birthday month

Key Experiences
in Movement

Moving in nonlocomotor ways

Moving in locomotor ways

Feeling and expressing steady bea

Ages 4-7

Apples, Peaches, Pears, and Plums

Children sit near one another and keep the steady beat while listening to the rhyme and reciting the 12 months of the year.

Apples, peaches, **pears**, and plums.
Tell us when your **birth**day comes.
January, **Feb**ruary, **March**, **A**pril, etc.

Materials

None

Activity to Experience

Children select a way to keep the steady beat and listen to the first two lines of the rhyme. Repeat these two lines several times so all the children can gradually join in speaking and moving.

Children recite the 12 months in order while keeping the steady beat. Pause after each month so each child can identify his or her birthday month by standing up. Continue to recite the months in order, keeping steady beat.

Facilitation and Reflection

How did you know when it was your turn to stand up?

How could we make the first two lines of the verse rhyme using other fruits or vegetables?

Extensions

Say the name of each month four times while keeping the beat: "**Jan**uary, **Jan**uary, **Jan**uary, **Jan**uary."

When the child stands, he or she freezes into a statue shape.

Children with the same birthday month join together and decide on a way to move about when they hear their birthday month. Recite the months again, pausing after each month to give children the opportunity to begin to move in their chosen way.

Curriculum Concepts

Steady beat

Swaying (rocking)

Rhyming words

Key Experiences in Movement

Moving in nonlocomotor ways

Feeling and expressing steady bea[t]

Ages 4-7

Boys and Girls Went Out to Play

Children keep the steady beat while swaying back and forth and chanting the rhyme.

Boys and girls went **out** to play,
Side to side **they** did sway.

Materials

None

Activity to Experience

Children are in short lines or in one semicircle. They keep the steady beat together while they listen to the rhyme and then join in saying the words.

Children talk about the meaning of the word "sway" and then try out different ways to sway. Several children take turns leading this activity.

The children choose a swaying movement and they all begin to keep the steady beat to it. Say the anchor word "sway" four times to bring all the children to synchronization with this beat, and then repeat the rhyme several times as a group. Suggest that the children change the swaying movement, and then chant the rhyme again to the steady beat.

Facilitation and Reflection

In what ways did we sway? Which way was most successful?

What are some other movement words that can be rhymed?

Extensions

Children can join together in some way and move to the swaying motion.

Older students can stand together and keep the beat.

Use two children's names instead of chanting "boys and girls." Have the two children lead the activity.

Encourage children to change the words, adding a different movement:

Boys and girls went **out** and hopped,
First they moved and **then** they stopped.

**Curriculum
Concepts**

Steady beat

Moving and speaking

Rhyming words

**Key Experiences
in Movement**

Moving in nonlocomotor ways

Moving in locomotor ways

Moving with objects

Feeling and expressing steady bea

Ages 4-7

Chocolate, Vanilla

Children explore movement inside their hoops.

Chocolate, vanilla, **take** a scoop;
Keep the beat in**side** your hoop.

Materials

One hoop for each child

Activity to Experience

Children find ways to move inside their hoops. Several children share their
movement ideas so the others can copy them. Also, they describe their
movements.

Demonstrate a steady beat movement and ask the children to copy. Then
ask, "Who else can show us a steady beat movement?" A child volunteers
a movement and all copy. Add the anchor word "beat" to the child's movement to bring all the children to synchronization and then say the rhyme.
Change the second line to "[Child's name] keeps the beat inside the hoop."

Children suggest other flavors of ice cream.

Facilitation and Reflection

How was Marla's steady beat movement different from Ben's movement?

What flavors of ice cream did we use in the rhyme?

Extensions

Work with movements in steady beat outside the hoops and contrast these with similar movements inside the hoops.

Work with movements in steady beat, like jumping or hopping, that can move "inside" and then "outside" the hoops. Change the words of the rhyme: "**Jump** into the hoop, **jump** out of the hoop; **in, out, in, out**."

Create additional two-line rhymes for steady beat.

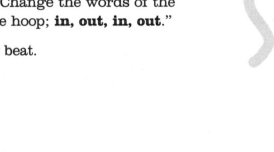

Curriculum
Concepts
Steady beat

Moving and speaking

Key Experiences
in Movement

Moving in nonlocomotor ways

Feeling and expressing steady be[a]

Ages 3-7

Feeling Beat

Children find ways to keep a silent steady beat and then, as a group, synchronize the movement while chanting the rhyme.

Feeling beat to**geth**er now;
Please join us; we'll **show** you how.
One steady beat **for** each word;
Silent beat so **it's** not heard.

Materials

None

Activity to Experience

Children explore ways to keep a silent steady beat with both hands. Volunteers share their ideas; the other children copy and then describe what they are doing.

Say the rhyme as the children keep the leader's silent steady beat. Say the rhyme several times so the children can join in as they wish.

Children choose a word they want to use at the end of the rhyme. (This could be a child's name, the name of a body part, a funny word, etc.) The word is said eight times at the end of the rhyme as you all keep the silent beat each time an accented word or accented syllable is spoken.

Facilitation and Reflection

What are some of the ways in which we kept a silent steady beat?

What was the hardest word to speak?

Extensions

Choose a sequence of two steady beat movements and two words to say along with them. (For each two beats in a line, the two movements in the sequence are used.) Put the two words together with the two beats in the sequence: "**Bend**, straighten **are** the words."

Keep steady beat off the body, e.g., shake or twist your hands.

Curriculum
Concepts

Steady beat

Moving and speaking

Key Experiences
in Movement

Moving in nonlocomotor ways

Feeling and expressing steady bea

Ages 5-7

Jack and Jill

Children explore swinging their arms back and forth. They chant the first verse of the rhyme to the steady beat while swinging their arms and chant the second verse, changing the tone of their voices for "'It hurts me,' so he said."

Jack and Jill went **up** the hill
To **fetch** a pail of **wa**ter.
Jack fell down and **broke** his crown,
And **Jill** came tumbling **af**ter.

Jack got up and **home** did go
And he **trav**eled oh so **slow.**
He **went** to bed with **ice** on his head,
"It **hurts** me," so he **said**.

Materials

None

Activity to Experience

Children explore swinging both arms from back to front slowly. One child is the leader and the others copy the movement in the child's steady beat tempo.

Say the first verse several times with different child leaders who each use their own tempo. Adjust the chanting to match each child's tempo.

Chant the second verse several times, allowing different children to lead. They change their voices for "It hurts me so."

Facilitation and Reflection

What did you notice about the steady beat as different children led the activity?

What problems were encountered as the tempo of the spoken rhyme was changed to match the leader's steady beat?

Extension

Use rhyming words for new verses the children create.

Change the movement from the swing and the step to different movements.

Younger children can keep steady beat for the verses in different ways by using two hands against the body.

**Curriculum
Concepts**

Steady beat

Locomotor concepts

Moving and speaking

**Key Experiences
in Movement**

Moving in locomotor ways

Feeling and expressing steady be[at]

Acting upon movement direction[s]

Ages 5-7

Jumping Joan

Children work with the two-line rhyme and perform the movements to the steady beat. The bold words and syllables underlined in the rhyme designate when the children land from the movement.

Here I <u>am</u>, little **jump**ing <u>Joan</u>.
When **no** one's <u>with</u> me, I'm **all** a<u>lone</u>.

Here I <u>am</u>, little **march**ing <u>Paul</u>.
First I'm <u>short</u>, and **then** I'm <u>tall</u>.

Here I <u>am</u>, little **hop**ping <u>Sue</u>.
As I <u>hop</u>, you **join** me <u>too</u>.

Here I <u>am</u>, little **jump**ing <u>Rose</u>.
Jump right <u>in</u>, and **hold** that <u>pose</u>.

Materials

None

Activity to Experience

Children keep steady beat and learn the first verse. They then explore different ways to jump. Several children share their movements and the other children describe them after they do them.

Children who suggest ideas also have their names used in the rhyme.

Learn another verse and encourage the children to explore that movement. Again, substitute a child's name for the name in the verse.

After two or three movements are explored, encourage the children to make up other verses that rhyme, writing them out for the others to see and learn.

Facilitation and Reflection

What different ways did we use to explore locomotor movement?

Was it difficult to combine the movement and the verse?

Extensions

Substitute nonlocomotor movements or action words so children can perform the verse while seated.

Jump as in jumping jacks to create a sequence of movements.

March four steps in and four steps out with the marching verse.

**Curriculum
Concepts**

Steady beat

Rhyming words

Moving and speaking

**Key Experiences
in Movement**

Moving in nonlocomotor ways

Feeling and expressing steady be

Ages 3-7

Mary Mack

Pat your knees to the steady beat and then have the children copy the movements, bringing them all to synchronization.

Mary Mack **dressed** in black.
Silver buttons **down** her back.
Hi-o, **hi**-o
Hi-o, hi-o, **hi**-o.

Kerry C. **dressed** in red.
Golden bows **on** her head.
(Repeat Hi-o line)

Materials

None

Activity to Experience

First have the children find their own ways to keep steady beat and to share their ideas with others. Choose one of the children's methods and bring all to synchronization using the anchor word "beat." Then recite the rhyme enough times so that all the children can become familiar with it and join in.

Children's first names should be substituted for "Mary": "**Ste**phanie Mack **dressed** in black," and they each become a leader. The child leaders choose the place on the body to keep steady beat.

Facilitation and Reflection

Where were some of the places we kept steady beat?

What other colors could we use in the rhyme and what rhymes with those colors?

Extensions

Five- to seven-year-old children can take a partner and sit one behind the other. The child in back pats steady beat on the shoulders of the child in front. The first name of the child in front is substituted for "Mary." The two children trade places and the rhyme is repeated.

Write new verses with preschool or early elementary children.

**Curriculum
Concepts**

Steady beat

Moving and speaking

Flow of speech

Opposites (up/down)

**Key Experiences
in Movement**

Moving in nonlocomotor ways

Feeling and expressing steady bea[t]

Ages 4-7
Piggy on the Railroad

Children stand and explore ways to move the entire body up and down as they chant the rhyme.

Piggy on the **rail**road **bend**ing up and **down**.
Along came an **eng**ine with **hard**ly any **sound**.
Piggy saw the **eng**ine and **let** out a **cry**.
"You **real**ly shouldn't **play** here," said the **eng**ine with a **sigh**.

Materials

None

Activity to Experience

Children keep the steady beat as you say the rhyme. At the end of the rhyme, ask the children about the story in the rhyme.

Children explore moving both parts of the upper body and the entire body up and down. Several children volunteer to share with the class the various ways they moved. Class members copy the bending and straightening movement of each volunteer and talk about it.

A child volunteers to be the leader. She begins by bending and straightening her knees. You say the corresponding anchor words "bend, straighten" four times and then chant the rhyme. Another child demonstrates a different bend-and-straighten movement and becomes the leader. The class does his movement (bending and straightening the arms) to the rhyme.

Facilitation and Reflection

What was Piggy doing on the railroad?

What did the train tell Piggy? Where are some places to play that are safe?

What were some of the ways we showed how to bend and straighten?

Extensions

Use a different pair of opposites, such as tall and short or in and out.

Choose a different place for Piggy, such as a street, and have a car or truck come along.

Choose another animal for the rhyme instead of Piggy.

Curriculum
Concepts

Steady beat

Opposites (up/down)

Moving and speaking

Key Experiences
in Movement

Moving in nonlocomotor ways

Moving with objects

Moving in sequences to a commo
beat

Feeling and expressing steady be

Ages 6-7

The Stretch Bands Blues

You introduce an up-and-down movement by pulling on a stretch band
that is anchored under one or both of your feet. After the children have
tried this movement, chant the rhyme, synchronizing their movements.

Up and down the **stretch** bands go,
Up and down, **move**ment is slow;
Pull and stretch is **what** you do,
Down they go, all the **way** to your shoe.

Materials

Stretch bands approximately one and a half inches wide and three feet long
formed into a loop

Activity to Experience

Children explore what they can do when holding a stretch band with one or
both hands. Several children volunteer to share their ideas so the others can
copy and then describe the movement.

Demonstrate an up-and-down movement by pulling a stretch band that you
have anchored under one or both feet. Demonstrate the movement using
one hand and one foot as well as using both hands for pulling and both feet
as the anchor for the band. Have children try the movement both ways and
discuss the differences.

All the children keep steady beat with their hands while you recite the rhyme several times. They join in when they are able to. They try the up-and-down movement without the stretch band as they say the first two lines of the rhyme. Children then try the slow upward movement on the third line of the rhyme and the slow downward movement on line four.

Decide on a way to pull the stretch band and have everyone begin to synchronize their movements. Add the anchor words "up, down" to the movement and chant the first two lines of the rhyme. Then stretch the bands upward slowly in a sustained movement and release them slowly for lines three and four.

Try other ways to move in opposite directions and alter the rhyme to fit the movements.

Facilitation and Reflection

How did the slow movement we used in the last part of the rhyme feel as compared to the movement in the first part?

What were some of the strategies you used to keep your movement synchronized with the others?

What were some of the opposites we used when we pulled the band?

Extensions

Younger children could just do the movements without the bands. Alter the words accordingly.

Have all the children use their whole body to go up and down to a steady beat and then to go up slowly and down slowly. Try using just arms or just legs for this purpose.

Curriculum
Concepts

Steady beat

Representation

Moving and speaking

Flow of speech

Key Experiences
in Movement

Moving in nonlocomotor ways

Feeling and expressing steady bea

Ages 4-7

Three Little Monkeys

Children find a way to swing like monkeys while reciting the rhyme. When they come to the last word, "snap," all the children show how they have decided to represent the crocodile.

Three little monkeys **swing**ing in a tree,
Along came a crocodile **qui**et as can be.
The **mon**keys said, "You **can't** catch me! "SNAP."

Materials

None

Activity to Experience

Children choose a swinging motion and bring the swing into synchronization as the adult says the anchor word "swing." Children match the beat with their swinging motions and listen to the rhyme. Say the rhyme several times to give all the children enough time to join in.

Children view a picture of a crocodile. Show them how you have seen a crocodile "snap" and ask how else they might represent this movement. Have several children share their ideas.

On the last word, "snap," all the children perform a snapping movement.

Facilitation and Reflection

How did some of the children do their snapping movement? How were they alike or different?

Why did the crocodile move quietly?

Why did the crocodile make a snapping movement?

Extensions

Younger children can keep the steady beat on some part of the body selected by one of them.

Children who have seen a crocodile might show how it moves.

Children who have not seen a crocodile can predict from the picture how it would move, and the other children can copy the movement.

Other animals or movements can be suggested by the children and the rhyme changed to fit.

Curriculum Concepts

Steady beat

Copying

Creative representation

Moving and speaking

Key Experiences in Movement

Moving in nonlocomotor ways

Moving in locomotor ways

Feeling and expressing steady beat

Expressing creativity in movement

Ages 4-7

The Train Went Into the Tunnel

Standing still, children pat the steady beat while you say the rhyme.
A child volunteer pretends to be the train going through the tunnel.
Upon leaving the tunnel, the child demonstrates a way for all to move.

The **train** went <u>in</u>to the **tun**nel ___,
To **see** what <u>it</u> could **see** ___.
When it came <u>out</u> of the **tun**nel ___,
It **moved** <u>a</u>round like **me** ___.

Materials

A "tunnel" made from a large carton (appliance size) with a hole at each end
or a blanket draped over a table.

Activity to Experience

Using both hands, children pat the steady beat against the body. Say an
anchor word to bring all the children to synchronization and then chant
the rhyme. Have the children try standing up and keeping the beat while
stepping.

Several children try simulating a train going through a tunnel. One child
volunteers to be the first "train" to go through the tunnel. The other children
keep the beat by patting or stepping, and they say the rhyme. (Add the
child volunteer's name in place of "me" at the end of the rhyme.)

At the end of the rhyme, the child leader comes out of the "tunnel" and shows a way to move around. The other children copy and describe the leader's movement.

Facilitation and Reflection

What were some of the ways children chose to go through the tunnel?

How does a real train travel?

Extensions

One child chooses a way for all to travel on the "train track" while they say the rhyme (e.g., shuffling, moving with small steps, galloping).

Younger children might crawl and not try to maintain the steady beat.

Have the entire group crawl through the tunnel.

Action Songs

Curriculum
Concepts
Steady beat

Space awareness

Moving and singing

Key Experiences
in Movement

Moving in locomotor ways

Feeling and expressing steady bea

Ages 4-7

All Around the Hula Hoop
(Pop Goes the Weasel)

Children explore different ways to travel around a large, marked circle area or around hoops placed on the floor, and they sing the song.

All around the **hu**la hoop,
The **child**ren now are **walk**-ing.
The **child**ren thought it was **all** in fun.
"**Pop**" and our **song** is done.

Materials

A hoop for each child (or one large circle marked on the floor)

Activity to Experience

Children explore different ways to travel around the outside of their hoops and share, copy, and describe several of their ideas.

Children step to the beat while the song is sung several times; they join in as they are able to.

Children select their favorite way to travel around the hoop or circle and all begin to move in this way. A steady beat and first pitch of the song are established, and all try to travel around the hoop or circle using the steady beat and singing the song.

Children notice the word "pop" near the end of the song. Ask the children what they might wish to do when that word is sung. Have children choose one of the several suggestions for movement to try out and include it in the words to the song.

Facilitation and Reflection

What ways to travel seem to fit the song the best?

What different ways to "pop" were demonstrated?

How did you know when to "pop"?

Extensions

All can follow one leader's way to travel around the hoops.

The song can be sung with younger children patting the beat but not being required to stay with the beat when they travel. Try to have them start moving to the beat, but realize that not all of them will have had enough experience to be totally successful.

Older students can travel around the space avoiding contact with the hoops. They can try to plan it so that they "pop" into a hoop at the right time.

Children can freeze into a statue shape after they "pop."

All Around the Hula Hoop

(Pop Goes the Weasel)

All a-round the hu – la hoop, The child - ren now are walk - ing. The

child – ren thought it was all in fun. Pop and our song is done.

Steady beat

Opposites (bend/straighten)

Sequences (patterns) of movement

Feeling and expressing steady beat

Moving in nonlocomotor ways

Moving in sequences to a common beat

Ages 3-7

Bend and Straighten Is the Game
(London Bridge Is Falling Down)

Children explore ways to bend and straighten their arms and legs as they sing the song.

Bend and **straight**-en **is** the **game**, **is** the **game**, **is** the **game**.
Bend and **straight**-en **is** the **game**.
Stop and **do** a **move**ment and **name**.

Materials

None

Activity to Experience

Children explore different ways to bend and straighten their arms and also their legs. Several children share their ideas, and they all copy and describe the movements.

A child volunteers to lead a bend and straighten movement for all to copy. Once the movement is started, add the song to match the child's bending and straightening movement.

During the last line of the song, all the children stop. Do a movement and have all the children copy and label your movement.

Children explore other ways to move and label their movement. A child volunteer leads the bending and straightening movement and adds a movement at the end.

Facilitation and Reflection

What were some of the ways we were bending and straightening? Were any harder? Easier?

What movement did we do at the end of the song?

Extensions

Single movements could be substituted for the sequence (pattern): "**Pat**ting **both** knees **is** the **game**."

Older children might enjoy the challenge at the end of the song of being given a label for the movement to do. Encourage children to think about how they will demonstrate that label.

Partners could synchronize the movement they choose at the end of the song.

Bend and Straighten Is the Game

(London Bridge Is Falling Down)

Bend and straight-en is the game, is the game, is the game. Bend and straight-en

is the game. Stop and do a move - ment and name.

Curriculum
Concepts

Steady beat

Opposites (in/out)

Moving and singing

Key Experiences
in Movement

Moving in nonlocomotor ways

Feeling and expressing steady bea

Acting upon movement directions

Ages 3-5

Everyone Keep the Beat
(Looby Loo)

Children keep the steady beat as they listen to the first two lines of the song. Then, as they listen to the movement directions of the next two lines, they do the movements as specified.

Everyone keep the **beat**. **Ev**eryone keep the **beat**.
Everyone keep the **beat**. **All** on a (Monday) **morn**ing.
We **put** our two hands **in**. We **put** our two hands **out**.
We **put** our two hands **in** again, and **wig**gle ourselves a**bout**.

Materials

None

Activity to Experience

A child volunteer begins keeping a steady beat by patting with both hands. All join in. Bring all the children to synchronization and sing the first two lines of the song several times, all the while encouraging the children to join in the singing.

Continue with the last two lines of the song, singing the directions for the children to follow. Pause after "in," after "out," and after "in again" to give children time to do the movement.

Before singing the song again, ask children to suggest other places on the body where they could pat the steady beat, and ask for more volunteers to lead the activity. Encourage children to suggest other spots where both hands could be placed.

Facilitation and Reflection

Where can we pat the steady beat against our bodies?

How did we move our hands away from our bodies?

Extensions

Older children can select pairs of opposites to sing about for verses two and three—up and down, together and apart.

Older children can perform a sequence of movements in steady beat during the first two lines of the song rather than doing one movement over and over: Knees, shoulders, head, shoulders.

Everyone Keep the Beat

(Looby Lou)

Curriculum
Concepts

Steady beat

Moving in general space

Responding to sung
directions

Key Experiences
in Movement

Moving in locomotor ways

Feeling and expressing steady beat

Acting upon movement directions

Ages 3-7

Gallop All Around

Children decide on a movement, perform it to the steady beat of the song,
and follow the directions at the end of the song.

Gallop, ga**ll**op, **gal**lop, ga**ll**op, **gal**lop <u>all</u> a**round** ___.
Gallop, ga**ll**op, **gal**lop, <u>put</u> your (**hands**) up<u>on</u> the **ground** ___.

Materials

None

Activity to Experience

Children are encouraged to keep a steady beat as the song is sung and
gallop about the room. They then decide on a different locomotor movement to do within the space and substitute that movement word for
"gallop" in the song.

As children begin the new locomotor movement, you can synchronize
the movement in steady beat and then sing the song.

At the end of the song, the sung direction, "Put your (hands) upon the
ground," can be changed to another movement by one of the children.

Facilitation and Reflection

What locomotor movements did we choose for traveling around the room?

What parts of the body did we touch the ground with at the end of the song?

What other movements might we try at the end of the song (e.g., hands in the air, elbows on our knees)?

Extensions

Older children can suggest rhyming words to sing on the ends of the lines.

Use nonlocomotor movements instead of locomotor ones.

Find ways to touch the ground with various parts of the body (elbows, head, thumbs).

Gallop All Around

Gal - op, gal - op, gal - op, gal - op, gal - op all a - round.

Gal - op, gal - op, gal - op, put your hands up - on the ground.

Steady beat

Space awareness ("how"—
big/little, loud/soft)

Moving and singing

Opposites (in/out)

Moving in locomotor ways

Feeling and expressing steady bea

Expressing creativity

Ages 4-7

Going Around Our Hoops
(Looby Loo)

Children explore different ways to move around the outside of their hoops and in and out of the hoops. They share their ideas and sing the song.

Going a<u>round</u> our **hoops** ___. (3 times)
All on a (<u>Mon</u>day) **morn**-ing.
We **jump** in<u>to</u> our **hoops** ___, we **jump** out of our **hoops** ___
We **jump** in<u>to</u> our **hoops** again, and **then** we jump back **out** ___.

Materials

A hoop for each child

Activity to Experience

Children find different ways to travel around the outside of their hoops. They share their ideas, and the other children copy and describe.

Children try different ways of moving into and out of their hoops or moving different parts of their body in and out of the hoop. Again, children share their ideas and the rest of the children copy.

One child leads and all follow. Add on the first part of the song. (*Note:* Do not make a conscious attempt to have younger children travel to the beat.) Several children lead while the song is sung. Encourage the children to join in the singing.

You may wish to try to have more experienced children travel to the beat of the music. If this is the case, bring all the children to synchronization with the leader's traveling beat by adding the first pitch of the song—singing it in steady beat (this is the anchor pitch).

To assess children's ability to follow directions, continue with the last part of the song using movements demonstrated by the children in the exploration phase of the activity.

Facilitation and Reflection

How did we travel around our hoop? What does it mean to go around?

How did Dale travel differently than Jacob?

What did we do to go into our hoops? Out of our hoops?

Extensions

All the children travel in their own way as the song is sung.

Children travel around the room and then find a hoop for the second part of the song.

Older students offer other ways to go around something, e.g., with a partner, a table, etc.

Going Around Our Hoops

(Looby Loo)

Go - ing a - round our hoops! Go - ing a - round our hoops!

Go - ing a - round our hoops! All on a (Mon - day) morn - ing. We jump in - to our

hoops. We jump out of our hoops. We jump in - to our hoops a - gain, and

then we jump back out.

Verse 2: We put our elbows in.
We put our elbows out.
We put our elbows in again
and then we take them out.

Steady beat

Space awareness ("how" and
"where")

Moving and singing

Moving in nonlocomotor ways

Feeling and expressing steady beat

Expressing creativity

Ages 3-7

Gonna Shake Out My Hands

Children explore different ways to shake their hands, then you sing the
song and the children respond to the song's directions.

Gonna (**shake**) out my (**hands**).
Gonna (**shake**) out my (**hands**).
Shake 'em high ___, **shake** 'em low ___,
Shake out my **hands**.

Materials

None

Activity to Experience

Children explore shaking their hands in different ways (e.g., fast and slow)
and in different spaces around the body (e.g., in front, up high).

Several children lead and the others copy and describe the movements.

Tell the children that you are going to sing a song about shaking their
hands and ask them to respond to the directions for how and where to
shake them. (*Note:* Be sure to pause in your singing after each direction to
give the children time to do the movement.)

Another way to do this activity is to have the children begin the shaking motion in steady beat while you use an anchor word to bring them all to synchronization and then sing the song.

Facilitation and Reflection

What were some of the ways we shook our hands? Where did we shake our hands?

How did you know where to put them when I sang the song?

Extensions

Use other ways and other places to shake the hands.

Choose other parts of the body to shake.

Use other action words besides shake for verses two and three.

Gonna Shake Out My Hands

Gon-na   shake out   my hands.   Gon - na   shake out   my hands.

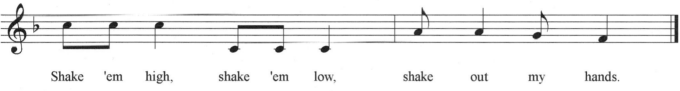

Shake   'em   high,   shake   'em   low,   shake   out   my   hands.

Verse 2:   Gonna wiggle my thumbs.
           Gonna wiggle my thumbs.
           Wiggle 'em up, wiggle 'em down,
           Wiggle my thumbs.

Verse 3:   Gonna dance with my fingers.
           Gonna dance with my fingers.
           Dance 'em up, dance 'em down,
           Dance with my fingers.

Curriculum
Concepts
Steady beat

Body awareness

Moving and singing

Key Experiences
in Movement

Moving in nonlocomotor ways

Feeling and expressing steady be[

Expressing creativity in moveme]

Ages 4-7

I Can Move One Foot
(Pretty Trappings)

Children explore moving only one foot (leg) and then explore moving only the other foot (leg). Children share their ideas. You establish the movements in steady beat and then sing the song.

I can **move** one **foot**, but the **oth**er is not **mov**ing.
I can **move** one **foot**, but the **oth**er can't be **moved**.
(Repeat with the other foot)

Materials

None

Activity to Experience

At large-group time, have the children lie on their backs and move both feet.

Then, have the children try moving only one foot (leg) and then the other foot. Initiate a movement for the children to try and then suggest that children find other positions and other ways to move only foot one at a time. Children share their discoveries.

Have the children do the movement using the SAY & DO process by saying "Foot, foot, foot, foot" as they move first one foot, then the other. When all the children are moving together, sing the song. Child volunteers can choose and lead other movements in steady beat.

Facilitation and Reflection

What were some different ways we moved our feet?

What different positions did we use?

Are there other parts of the body that we could use instead of one of our feet?

Extensions

Substitute hand (arm) or other parts of the body suggested by the children and sing the song.

Substitute two parts of the body that can move symmetrically.

Try changing the words:

I can **march** all a**round** ____, **and** my feet keep **mov**ing.
I can **march** all a**round** ____, and **then** my body **stops** ____.

I Can Move One Foot

(Pretty Trappings)

Traditional Tune

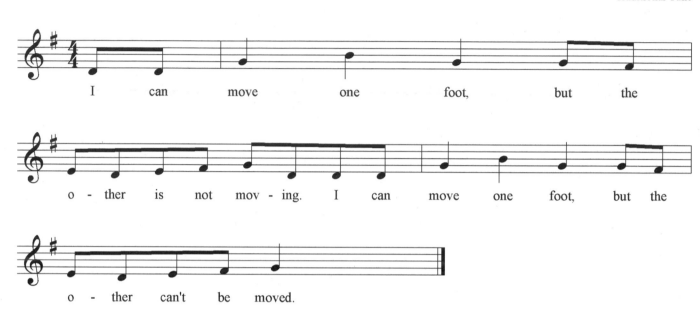

I can move one foot, but the o - ther is not mov - ing. I can move one foot, but the o - ther can't be moved.

Verse 2:   I can move the other foot,
           but the first one is not moving.
           I can move the other foot,
           but the first one can't be moved.

Curriculum
Concepts

Steady beat

Awareness of personal and
general space

Listening and responding

Emotions (happy, sleepy, sad)

Key Experiences
in Movement

Moving in nonlocomotor ways

Acting upon movement directions

Expressing creativity in movement

Ages 4-7

If You're Happy (Variation)

Children show ways to convey happiness by moving their arms, legs, face,
and every place. They respond to the song's directions.

If you're **hap**py and you **know** it, show it **with** your **arms**!
If you're **hap**py and you **know** it, show it **with** your **legs**!
If you're **hap**py and you **know** it, show it **in** your **face**!
If you're **hap**py and you **know** it, show it **every place**!

Materials

None

Activity to Experience

Children explore many ways to convey happiness through their movements.

Children talk about the word "happy" and what makes them happy.

Several children volunteer to share how they can show happiness by moving different parts of their body while seated.

Explain to the children that you will sing a song that has ways for them to
show happiness with their arms, legs, face, and all over (every place). Sing

the song, pausing at the end of each line (musical phrase) to give children the opportunity to express happiness.

Facilitation and Reflection

What movements did we choose for showing happiness?

What parts of the body were used to show happiness?

When are we "happy"?

What other ways (emotions) might we sing about in each line (phrase) of the song?

Extensions

Show the meaning of other words (sleepy, angry) with movement.

Move the arms in a specific direction at the end of each phrase (arms up high, down low, to the side, turning around and around). Ask the children for other ideas.

If You're Happy

If you're hap - py and you know it, show it

with your arms! If you're hap - py and you know it, show it

with your legs! If you're hap - py and you know it, show it

in your - face! If you're hap - py and you know it, show it

ev - 'ry place.

**Curriculum
Concepts**

Steady beat

Time awareness (fast, slow)

Moving and singing

**Key Experiences
in Movement**

Moving in locomotor ways

Feeling and expressing steady bea

Ages 4-7

Jump, Everybody
(Hop Old Squirrel)

Children explore marching, jumping, and hopping movements. One child selects one of the movements and all copy. You sing the song to the child's timing.

Jump, every**body**, **eid**le dum, **eid**le dum.
Jump, every**body**, **eid**le dum **dee** ___. (Repeat song)

Materials

None

Activity to Experience

Children explore locomotor movements at outside time. You notice that some of the children are copying one another. (You could also suggest similar activities for the children to do so you could introduce the song activity later in the daily routine.)

During large-group time, ask for a child volunteer to demonstrate the marching, jumping, or hopping they were doing during outside time. The other children copy the leader and you sing the song.

The children think of other nonsense words to use instead of "eidle dum."

Facilitation and Reflection

What were some different ways we moved our feet?

What other words did we use instead of "eidle dum?"

Extensions

Substitute nonlocomotor movement: "**Swing** both **arms**, **eid**le dum, **eid**le dum," or "**Pound** our **legs**, **eid**le dum, **eid**le dum."

Have the children select four parts of the body to use in the song:

Hands on your **shoul**ders, **eid**le dum, **eid**le dum.
Hands on your **head**, **eid**le dum, **dee**.
Hands on your **knees**, **eid**le dum, **eid**le dum.
Hands on your **ears**, **eid**le dum **dee**.

Jump, Everybody

(Hop Old Squirrel)

Traditional Tune

Jump, ev'-ry-bo - dy, ei - dle-dum, ei - dle-dum. Jump, ev'-ry-

bo - dy, ei - dle-dum dee. Jump, ev'-ry-bo - dy, ei - dle-dum, -

ei - dle-dum. Jump ev'-ry-bo - dy, ei - dle-dum dee.

Verse 2:   Hands on your shoulders, eidle dum, eidle dum.
Hands on your head, eidle dum dee.
Hands on your knees, eidle dum, eidle dum.
Hands on your ears, eidle dum dee.

**Curriculum
Concepts**
Steady beat

Patting movements

**Key Experiences
in Movement**

Moving in nonlocomotor ways

Feeling and expressing steady beat

Ages 3-7

Let Everyone Keep the Beat
(Let Everyone Clap Hands With Me)

Children follow the leader in a steady movement—patting on the chest
with two hands. Children pat other places on the body and lead the group
in singing the song to the patting motion.

Let **ev**eryone keep the **beat**. (Repeat)
Come **on** now and join in the **game**.
You'll **find** that it's always the **same**.

Materials

None

Activity to Experience

Begin a steady movement by patting both hands against your chest.
Encourage the children to follow your lead and touch their chests at the
same time you do. Sing the song, patting on the bold words or syllables.

The children use both hands to pat other places on their bodies. Suggest
that they share their ideas and have the class copy their movements. After
a child begins a new movement, say "Beat, beat, beat, beat" in time with the
child's movement, then sing the song.

As each child leader begins a movement, the others copy. Sing the word,
"beat," four times using the starting pitch of the song (anchor pitch).

Children can sing the song as they become familiar with the words and the melody.

Facilitation and Reflection

What parts of the body did we use for keeping the steady beat?

What do we mean by steady beat?

Why was it more difficult to keep the beat while singing the song?

Extensions

Change the words to "**Ev**eryone keep beat with **Joe**." (Use the child leader's name.)

All the children keep the steady beat in a place of their own choosing.

Try adding just an auditory cue. Ask everyone to find a place to keep steady beat and then add the starting pitch. Children match the tempo of the anchor pitch.

Keep the beat with an object (e.g., lumee sticks, PVC pipe, or cardboard paper towel holders).

Let Everyone Keep the Beat

(Let Everyone Clap Hands With Me)

Folk Song

Let e - v' - ry one keep the beat. Let e - v' - ry one keep the

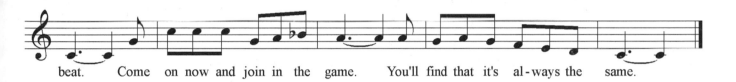

beat. Come on now and join in the game. You'll find that it's al - ways the same.

Curriculum Concepts

Steady beat

Creative representation

Moving and singing

Key Experiences in Movement

Moving in locomotor ways

Expressing creativity in movemer

Feeling and expressing steady be

Ages 4-7

Monster, Monster, Monster Man
(Row, Row, Row Your Boat)

Children talk about things that are scary. A child begins to move in a scary way and the other children copy. Then they sing the song with you.

Monster, monster, **mon**ster man, **walk** around the **space** ___.
Oo Oo **Oo** Oo, **it's** a scary **place** ___.

Materials

None

Activity to Experience

Children talk about things that are scary. Once a child begins to move in a scary way, the other children follow.

When asked, a child says he is a "monster." As he begins to move again, you can sing the song.

Encourage other children to explore how a monster might move about. They volunteer to share and all follow and talk about the way each child volunteer is moving. With each volunteer, sing the song to the beat set by the child.

Facilitation and Reflection

What does it mean to move like a monster?

How were the monster ways different?

Extensions

Children move as other characters in books.

Children find other ways to move about the space, e.g., down low or up high.

Children move as they have seen objects move, e.g., balls, swings, etc.

Monster, Monster, Monster Man

(Row, Row, Row Your Boat)

Mon - ster, mon - ster, mon - ster man, Walk a - round the space.

Oo - oo - oo - oo - It's a sca - ry place.

Verse 2: Pumpkin, pumpkin, pumpkin bright,
Roll around the space.

Verse 3: Ghost, ghost, goblin ghost,
Float around the space.

Verse 4: Witches, witches on your brooms,
Gallop 'round the space.

Verse 5: Boney, boney, boney man,
Jump around the space.

**Curriculum
Concepts**

Steady beat

Turning (arms going around)

Moving and singing

**Key Experiences
in Movement**

Moving in nonlocomotor ways

Expressing creativity in movement

Ages 3-7

My Hands Keep Moving

Children explore moving their hands and arms in various ways and then copy one child's movement as a group. You start to sing the song so the children can join in.

All **day** my hands keep **mov**-ing, keep **mov**-ing, keep **mov**-ing.
All **day** my hands keep **mov**-ing, **'round** and 'round like **this**.

Materials

None

Activity to Experience

Children find different ways to move their hands, e.g., shaking, pounding.

Children share their discoveries as leaders of the activity. All copy the leader and then sing the song.

If the movement can be put into steady beat, use an anchor word, in the first pitch of the song, to match the movement ("around, around, around, around") before you sing the song.

If children are also singing, sing the starting pitch in steady beat.

Facilitation and Reflection

How did we move our hands with the song?

What other parts of the body could we move?

What are some of the movements our feet could do?

Extensions

Make a list of the ways of moving children suggested.

School-aged children can explore movements and share their ideas in small groups.

Make comparisons as to "where" and "how" the same movement was used, (in front, overhead, big, little).

My Hands Keep Moving

All day my hands keep mo - ving, keep mov - ing, keep mov - ing. All day my hands keep

mov - ing 'round and 'round like this.

Curriculum
Concepts

Steady beat

Body awareness

Moving and singing

Key Experiences
in Movement

Moving in nonlocomotor ways

Feeling and expressing steady be

Ages 3-7

Our Fingers and Thumbs Keep Moving
(One Finger, One Thumb)

Children discover ways to keep steady beat as they move their fingers and thumbs at the same time and sing the song with you.

Our **fin**gers and thumbs keep **mov**-ing,
Our **fin**gers and thumbs keep **mov**-ing,
Our **fin**gers and thumbs keep **mov**-ing,
They're **mov**-ing and then they **stop**.

Materials

None

Activity to Experience

Show children a way to move the fingers and thumbs all at once. Once the children copy, add the anchor pitch to the movement to try to establish a common beat and first pitch of the song before singing the song.

Encourage children to find another way to move their fingers and thumbs. Ask for a child leader and have the other children copy the leader's movements. Then sing the song to the child leader's steady beat.

Encourage the children to choose another body part to add to the finger and thumb movement so that they are moving three body parts at the same time.

Facilitation and Reflection

How did we move our fingers and thumbs at the same time?

What did you do to move all the fingers and thumbs together?

What other parts of the body did we use for the song?

Extensions

For younger children, begin by using only fingers or thumbs.

Have older children suggest where they can do the movement, e.g., up high, down low, etc.

Begin by using a different pair of body parts in the song, such as feet or elbows.

Our Fingers and Thumbs Keep Moving

(One Finger, One Thumb)

Our   fin - gers   and thumbs   keep   mo - ving. Our   fin - gers   and thumbs   keep   mo - ving. Our

fin - gers   and thumbs   keep   mo -   ving. They're   mo - ving and then they   stop

Verse 2:   Our fingers and thumbs and arms keep moving.

Verse 3:   Our fingers and thumbs and arms and legs keep moving.

Steady beat

Body awareness

One-step directions

Moving in nonlocomotor ways

Feeling and expressing steady beat

Acting upon movement directions

Ages 5-7

Pat Your Chin and Not Your Hair

(Jimmy Crack Corn)

Children watch and copy as you slowly pat your chin. Sing the song after all the children are keeping the steady beat with you.

Pat your **chin** and **not** your **hair**. (3 times)
Pat it a**gain** and **stop now**.

Materials

None

Activity to Experience

Children watch and copy as you slowly pat your chin. Add the anchor word "pat" to try to bring all the children into a synchronized beat before singing the song.

After you ask the children to name the place they are patting and where they are not patting, encourage them to choose other places to pat and not to pat. For example, one child may suggest patting shoes and another may say not to pat socks. Add these words to the song.

Encourage children to plan other places to pat and not pat and also to join in singing the song.

Facilitation and Reflection

What places did we pat and not pat? How did you know not to pat your hair or your socks?

What other parts of the body did we mention in the song?

Extensions

Move parts of the body rather than patting them.

Instead of using the phrase "and not your hair," substitute a way to pat, such as softly: "**Pat** your **chin soft**-ly **now**."

Substitute walking rather then patting.

Just pat, singing "**Pat** your **chin**, **pat** with **Al**-ex."

Pat Your Chin and Not Your Hair

(Jimmy Crack Corn)

Pat your chin and not your hair.   Pat your chin   and not your hair.   Pat your chin and

not   your   hair.   Pat   it   a - gain   and   stop   now.

Verse 2:   One hand up in the air,
            Other hand in the air,
            Both hands up in the air,
            Bring them down,
            and pat your knees!

Curriculum
Concepts
Steady beat

Body awareness

Action words

Key Experiences
in Movement

Moving in nonlocomotor ways

Feeling and expressing steady bea

Ages 3-7

Ritsch, Ratsch

A child leader pounds his fists slowly on his upper legs; the other children copy the movements. You add the anchor word "boom" with each pound and then sing the song.

Ritsch, **ratsch**, fi li **boom**, boom, **boom**,
Fi li **boom**, boom, **boom**, fi-li **boom**, boom, **boom**.
(Repeat the two lines.)

Materials

None

Activity to Experience

At large-group time, begin pounding your fists on your legs using both hands and encourage all the children to do the same. Then sing the song, encouraging all the children to join in.

The funny words of the song will capture the children's attention, enabling you to encourage all the children to pound their legs as you say "pound, pound, pound, pound" without singing. Then sing the song again so the children can join in on the "boom, boom, boom" part. (*Note:* The pounding motion occurs only the first and third "boom.") Children can also lead the activity.

Children find other parts of the body or the floor to pound.

Facilitation and Reflection

What places did we use to pound our fists?

What does it mean to pound?

What other silly words could we use instead of "boom, boom, boom?"

How did it feel when we pounded other places?

Extensions

Use other action words as the child leaders suggest new movements.

Change the song to a rhyme and have older children (five–seven years of age) chant the rhyme with a partner. If they are all comfortable with this, have them try to sing the song in pairs.

Make up other silly songs to the melody.

Ritsch, Ratsch

Ritsch, ratsch, fi - li - boom, boom, boom, fi - li - boom, boom, boom, fi - li -

boom, boom, boom. Ritsch, ratsch, fi - li - boom, boom, boom, fi - li -

boom, boom, boom, fi - li - boom, boom, boom.

Curriculum
Concepts

Steady beat

Rocking back and forth

Moving and singing

Key Experiences
in Movement

Moving in nonlocomotor ways

Feeling and expressing steady beat

Ages 5-7

Rock, Rock, Rock Your Boat
(Row, Row, Row Your Boat)

Children pretend that they are all in a boat and that the boat is rocking back and forth. They begin to rock and a child leader adds the anchor word "rock," saying it four times. Then the child leader begins to sing the song.

Rock, rock, **rock** your boat, **gent**ly back and **forth**.
Merrily, merrily, **mer**rily, merrily, **we** go back and **forth**.

Materials

Broom handles or poles

Activity to Experience

Groups of four children sit between two poles and hold on. They are pretending to be in a boat. They explore moving side-to-side together in their "boat."

Start the children rocking back and forth. After they are moving together, say "rock, rock, rock, rock" and begin singing the song. (The rocking movement occurs only on the first and third "rocks.")

Children explore other ways to move together in their pretend boats and share their ideas with the class. Sing the song to their movements and change the words to fit the movement being demonstrated.

Facilitation and Reflection

How did you all rock together?

What does rocking mean?

What other movements did you do together? Were they as successful as your rocking movement?

What would happen if our groups had more people in them?

Extensions

Have larger groups rock or use other movements in a synchronized way.

Try rocking while standing up between the poles.

Think of other boats and how you might make them move. Simulate these movements.

Rock, Rock, Rock Your Boat

(Row, Row, Row Your Boat)

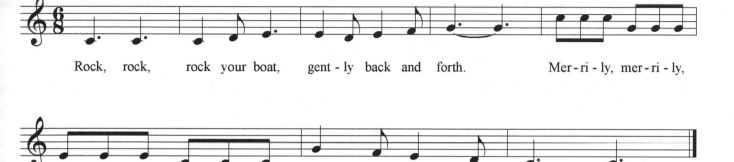

Rock, rock, rock your boat, gent - ly back and forth. Mer - ri - ly, mer - ri - ly,

mer - ri - ly, mer - ri - ly, we go back and forth.

Curriculum
Concepts
Steady beat

Action word (shake)

Moving and singing

Key Experiences
in Movement

Moving in nonlocomotor ways

Feeling and expressing steady be

Ages 3-7

Shake to My Lou
(Skip to My Lou)

Children shake both hands in front of the body and do the motion to a steady beat using the anchor word "shake." Then they sing the song.

Shake, shake, **shake** to my Lou. (3 times)
Shake to my Lou and **stop** sign.

Materials

None

Activity to Experience

Invite the children to join you in shaking both hands in front of the body. After the children have joined in, say the anchor words "shake, shake, shake, shake" to bring all of them together in steady beat and then sing the song.

Ask the children where else they could shake both hands. When a child makes a suggestion, sing the song with the new movement and substitute the child's name for "Lou": "**Shake**, shake, **shake** with Robin." Other children volunteer to be the leader and the activity continues as long as the children seem interested. (*Note:* There are only two movements—on the first and third shake.)

Ask if the children could think of other movements to do, and sing the song accordingly.

Facilitation and Reflection

What were the various places we used for shaking our hands?

What does it mean to shake our hands?

What other movements did we use?

What could we do if we were standing?

Extensions

Older children can be partners with one deciding where to shake the hands. Each pair of partners substitutes the name of the child leader for "Lou."

Older children can skip as in the original version of the song.

In this case the skipping movement occurs with each "skip" and with "Lou" (four skips per line).

Younger children might be more successful doing an action against the body, such as patting.

Shake to My Lou

(Skip to My Lou)

Traditional Tune

Shake, shake, shake to my Lou. Shake, shake, shake to my Lou.

Shake, shake, shake to my Lou, shake to my Lou and stop sign.

(my dar- ling)

*Curriculum
Concepts*
Steady beat

Spatial awareness (using
locomotor movement)

Moving and singing

*Key Experiences
in Movement*

Moving in locomotor ways

Feeling and expressing steady beat

Expressing creativity in movement

Ages 3-7

Special Place
(Here We Go 'Round the Mulberry Bush)

Children plan a way to go around their shape or hoop. They talk about their plan. While they are moving, you sing the song. When they go around their hoop or shape again, establish a steady beat so the children can move to it.

Go a<u>round</u> your **spe**<u>cial</u> <u>place</u>, **spe**<u>cial</u> <u>place</u>, **spe**<u>cial</u> <u>place</u>.
Go a<u>round</u> your **spe**<u>cial</u> <u>place</u>, **then** <u>you</u> **rest** ___.

Materials

A shape or hoop for each child

Activity to Experience

Children move around their own special shapes. As they move around the shape, you sing the song.

Encourage the children to make a plan for the way they will travel around their shapes. Have them describe the way they are going to move. Again, you add the song.

A child volunteer demonstrates a way of traveling. Encourage the other children to copy the child leader's movement. As the leader begins, use a word that matches the child's beat. Sing the song after helping the children establish a common beat.

Other children volunteer to lead.

Facilitation and Reflection

What were some of the ways we went around our special place?

What do we mean by the word "around"?

How was [the child leader's] way different from [another child leader's] way?

What could we go around in our classroom?

Extensions

Children go around all the shapes.

Children choose locomotor movement for traveling.

Children change the words of the song:

Nathan said to **march** around, **march** around, **march** around.
Nathan said to **march** around, **who** is **next** ____?

Special Place

(Here We Go Round the Mulberry Bush)

Go a - round your spe - cial place, spe - cial place, spe - cial place.

Go a - round your spe - cial place then you rest.

Verse 2: Match the statue that you see,
 that you see, that you see.
 Match the statue that you see.
 and be still.

Verse 3: Nathan said to march around.
 march around, march around.
 Nathan said to march around,
 Who is next_____?

Curriculum
Concepts
Steady beat

Swinging

Moving and singing

Key Experiences
in Movement

Moving in nonlocomotor ways

Feeling and expressing steady be

Ages 3-7

Swing Your Arms
(Row, Row, Row Your Boat)

Children watch and join in a swinging movement you are doing. Everyone stops and describes your swinging movement. One child begins the swing again and all copy. You add the anchor word "swing" to the child's established beat and then begin to sing the song.

Swing, swing, **swing** your arms.
Swing them back and **forth**.
Swing, swing, **swing** your arms.
Swing them both and **stop**.

Materials

None

Activity to Experience

Encourage the children to join you in swinging both arms back and forth (front to back)—in the same way as you observed one of the children doing at outside time. Ask the children to talk about what they noticed about your swinging movements.

Begin the movement again and have the children copy it. Sing the anchor pitch "swing" four times and then sing the song to your established steady beat. (*Note:* There are only two "swing" motions—on the first and the third "swing" words.)

Encourage children to lead the activity. As one child leads, sing the anchor pitch to that child's beat before singing the song.

Facilitation and Reflection

What does it mean to swing our arms?

What is another way we could swing our arms?

Is there anything else we could swing?

Extensions

Have children use other nonlocomotor words, such as "twist," "turn," "flap."

Locomotor words may be substituted: "We 'march,' 'walk,' 'jump,' 'skate.'"

When locomotor concepts are used, the walking beat becomes—

March, march, **march** your feet.
March them just like **this** ___.
March, march, **march** your feet.
March them now and **stop** ___.

Children might suggest joining hands to swing.

Swing Your Arms
(Row, Row, Row Your Boat)

Swing, swing, swing your arms. Swing them back and forth. Swing, swing,

swing your arms. Swing them both and stop.

Verse 2: March, march, march your feet.
March them just like this.
March, march, march your feet.
March them now and stop.

Verse 3: Turn, turn, turn your arms.
Turn them all around.
Turn, turn, turn your arms.
Turn them now and stop.

Curriculum
Concepts
Steady beat

Moving and singing

Key Experiences
in Movement

Moving in nonlocomotor ways
Feeling and expressing steady beat
Acting upon movement directions

Ages 3-7

This Is What I Can Do

The children are playing outside, and one child is observed bending his knees in steady beat. Call attention to what the child is doing and have the other children join in. Other children lead with other movements. Sing the song with the leader's name in it.

This is what **I** can do. **See** if you can **do** it too.
This is what **I** can do. **Now** I'll pass it **on** to you.

Materials

None

Activity to Experience

The children bend their knees in a steady movement. When all the children are doing the movement, say the anchor word "knees" four times and sing the song.

Encourage the other children to lead using other movements. When a child volunteers, add the appropriate anchor word to the movement and then sing the song using the child's name instead of "I."

Facilitation and Reflection

What movement did Isabel do? What movement did Jacob do? How were they different?

What other movements could we do with the song?

Extensions

Use a sequence of steady beat movements, such as bend-straighten or up-down.

With older children, change the words in the song:

Our arms go **in** and out. **First** they go in, **then** they go out.
Our arms go **in** and out. **What** else can you **call** in-out?

Use locomotor movements—tiptoe, walking on heels, big steps

This Is What I Can Do

This is what I can do. See if you can do it too.

This is what I can do. Now I'll pass it on to you!

Curriculum
Concepts
Steady beat

Moving and singing

Wiggling movement

Key Experiences
in Movement

Moving in nonlocomotor ways

Feeling and expressing steady be

Expressing creativity in moveme:

Ages 3-7

Thumbs Go Wiggle Waggle

Children copy you as you wiggle both thumbs in front of your body.
Children find other places in which to wiggle the thumbs and suggest other
parts of the body that can wiggle. All respond to the song's directions.

Thumbs go **wig**gle-waggle, **wig**gle-waggle, **wig**gle-waggle
Thumbs go **wig**gle-waggle, **then** they **stop**.

Materials

None

Activity to Experience

Wiggle both thumbs in front of your body and encourage the children to
copy. Label the action "wiggle-waggle."

Sing the song after providing an anchor word, such as "beat" to bring all
together in steady beat.

Encourage the children to find other places to wiggle-waggle their thumbs,
such as to the side, on the head, under the knees. Ask the children to volunteer to lead the activity.

Choose other parts of the body to wiggle-waggle, and alter the words of the
song to fit.

Facilitation and Reflection

What are your thumbs doing when they wiggle?

Where were some of the places we wiggle-waggled?

What other body parts are easy to wiggle-waggle? Hard to wiggle-waggle?

What else have we seen wiggle?

Extensions

Children suggest other action words and add a silly second word to each (such as "jiggle-giggle").

Substitute "just like [child's name]" at the end of the song.

Change the placement of the action at the end of the song.

For less experienced children, wiggle the thumbs without using a specific steady beat.

Thumbs Go Wiggle Waggle

Thumbs go wig - gle wag - gle, wig - gle wag - gle, wig - gle wag - gle.

Thumbs go wig - gle - wag - gle, then they stop.

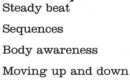
Steady beat

Sequences

Body awareness

Moving up and down

Moving in nonlocomotor ways

Feeling and expressing steady beat

Acting upon movement directions

Ages 4-7

Tommy Thumb

Children play follow-the-leader with you. Pause after each movement so the children can identify each placement. Sing the song when the children appear to be comfortable with the movements.

Tommy Thumb is **up**, and **Tommy** Thumb is **down**.
Tommy Thumb is **dan**cing, **all** around the **town**.
Dance them on your **shoul**ders. **Dance** them on your **head**.
Dance them on your **knees**, and **tuck** them into **bed**.

Materials

None

Activity to Experience

The children are playing a follow-the-leader game with you. Put your two thumbs up and pause, then down and pause. Have the children do the movements on their own as you say the words "up" and "down."

Ask the children to "dance the thumbs all around." Then review the sequence "up, down, dancing all around" and sing the song.

Follow this by having the children copy your movements again: two beats on the shoulder performed slowly, two beats on the head, and finally two beats on the knees before "tucking them into bed." Have the children decide

how they will "tuck them into bed." Have the children review the order of the steady beat on shoulders, head, and knees using the SAY & DO process: "Shoulders, shoulders, head, head, knees, knees." Continue with the second part of the song.

The children now see if they can recall what movement comes first, next, and so on, from the beginning of the song. Sing the entire song while the children do the movements.

Facilitation and Reflection

How did you make your thumbs dance?

Are there any other parts of the body we could use in the song?

What places on the body did we use to keep the steady beat?

Extensions

The children can choose both the order and the parts of the body to use in the second part of the song.

Try "**All** the fingers **up** and **all** the fingers **down**, etc."

Use elbows, feet, and other body parts for up and down.

Tommy Thumb

Tom - my Thumb is up and Tom - my Thumb is down.

Tom - my Thumb is danc - ing all a - round the town.

Dance him on your shoul - ders. Dance him on your head.

Dance him on your knees, and tuck him in - to bed.

Verse 2:   Put your two arms up
And put your two arms down.
Make your two arms do a
dance all around the town.
Straighten them in front,
and straighten them in back.
Bend them to the sides
and now you lay them flat.

Curriculum
Concepts

Steady beat

Locomotor movement labels

Spatial awareness: moving
around objects

Key Experiences
in Movement

Moving in locomotor ways

Feeling and expressing steady be

Expressing creativity in moveme

Ages 4-7

Walk Around the Chairs Today

(Mary Had a Little Lamb)

Children explore ways to walk around their chairs, share their ways
of moving, and describe them. They sing the song to the leader's
way of walking.

Walk ar<u>ound</u> the **chairs** to<u>day</u>,
chairs to<u>day</u>, **chairs** to<u>day</u>.
Walk ar<u>ound</u> the **chairs** to<u>day</u>,
and **then** we <u>all</u> sit **down** ___.

Materials

A chair, hula hoop, or carpet square for each child

Activity to Experience

Children find different ways to travel around their chairs (or hula hoops,
or carpet squares). Sing the song while the children are moving around
the objects.

Children volunteer to be the leader. Each child leader demonstrates a special
way of moving and the other children copy and describe. The leader tells
the group what the movement is called and that word is substituted for
"walk" in the song.

The leader begins the movement, the children copy, and you say the anchor word "march" (word chosen by the child leader) four to eight times before beginning to sing the song in the child's "marching" beat.

Facilitation and Reflection

What does it mean to "go around"?

How did you know how to move your feet to the steady beat?

What ways did we go around our chairs?

Extensions

Change the words to "**Gallop** around the **chairs** today. . . ".

Step in place, changing the song to "**Step** our feet **right** in place."

Preschool children: Place the child's symbol and name on the chairs. The children walk around all the chairs. When the singing stops they find their own chair with the appropriate symbol and name on it.

Kindergarten and first grade: Using file cards, put a card with a child's name on each chair. Do the same activity, and have each of the children find their name at the end of the song.

Walk Around the Chairs Today

(Mary Had a Little Lamb)

Walk a - round the chairs to - day, chairs to - day,

chairs to - day. Walk a - round the chairs to - day, and

then we all sit down.

Verse 2: Gallop around the chairs today,
chairs today, chairs today.
Gallop around the chairs today,
and then we all sit down.

Curriculum
Concepts

Steady beat

Body awareness

Key Experiences
in Movement

Moving in nonlocomotor ways

Feeling and expressing steady beat

Acting upon movement directions

Ages 3-7

We Can Keep a Steady Beat
(Muffin Man)

Children watch and copy a child leader who puts her hands on her knees. She keeps steady beat on her knees during the song. Other children choose other places to pat and then lead the song.

We can **keep** a **stead**y **beat**, a **stead**y **beat**, a **stead**y **beat**.
We can **keep** a **stead**y **beat**, **(Kar**en) **find** the **next place**.

(Karen) **keeps** a **stead**y **beat**, a **stead**y **beat**, a **stead**y **beat**.
(Karen) **keeps** a **stead**y **beat**, **who** will **find** the **next place**.

Materials

None

Activity to Experience

Put both hands on your head and ask the children to copy and identify where they put their hands. Begin a steady beat and then sing the song.

Choose a child's movement for all to copy (both hands on the knees, for example). Then ask the child leader to keep a steady beat that is slow, so you can sing a song. Begin by singing the anchor pitch "knees" four times in the child's beat, then begin singing the song.

Ask the children where else they could keep a steady beat and select a child volunteer to be the leader. Keep the steady beat and sing the song.

Facilitation and Reflection

What does it mean to keep steady beat?

Where was it easy to keep steady beat? Hard?

What were some of the places on the body we used to pat the steady beat?

Extensions

Keep the steady beat with nonlocomotor movements, such as twist or swing.

Keep the steady beat with objects, such as sticks or paper plates.

Older children: Keep movement sequences in steady beat, such as bend and straighten, up and down.

We Can Keep a Steady Beat

(Muffin Man)

We can keep a stea - dy beat, a

stea - dy beat, a stea - dy beat.

We can keep a stea - dy beat.

(Kar - en) find the next place.

Verse 2 :   (Karen) keeps a steady beat,
a steady beat, a steady beat.
(Karen) keeps a steady beat,
(Connie) find the next place.

Verse 3:   (Connie) keeps a steady beat,
a steady beat, a steady beat.

Ages 4-7

We Walk Our Feet

Children explore different ways to walk their feet and then sing the song while moving.

We <u>walk</u> our **feet** (<u>toes</u> **in**).
We <u>walk</u> our **feet** (<u>toes</u> **in**),
We <u>walk</u> our **feet** (<u>toes</u> **in**),
and <u>then</u> we **stop**.

Materials

None

Activity to Experience

Encourage children to find different ways to walk their feet by first showing them "toes in" as one way. They all try this way, talk about it, and then find other ways to walk their feet.

Children volunteer to lead the activity and suggest new ways to walk their feet. The others copy and describe what the leader is doing with his or her feet.

Sing the song using "toes in" instead of "feet." Have everyone walk this way as they say "walk" several times using the SAY & DO process, and then sing the song again. At the end of the song, freeze. Ask the children to talk about what happened at the end of the song.

Encourage other children to lead and to tell everyone what they want to call their special walk. Then add their words to the song.

Facilitation and Reflection

"What was the special way I was walking my feet?" "What did [child's name] do with her feet?"

What was an easy way to walk? Hard way?

What happened at the end of the song? How did we keep ourselves from falling down?

Extensions

Older children: Walk with a partner and synchronize movements.

Use the words "gallop" and "skip" and say them again at the ends of phrases: "We (skip) our **feet** (skip, **skip**)."

The leader makes a statue shape at the end of the song and all copy.

We Walk Our Feet

We walk our feet (toes in), we walk our

feet (toes in), we walk our feet (toes in), and then we

stop.

About the Author

Phyllis S. Weikart, Director of the Movement and Music Division, High/Scope Foundation, and developer of the program "Education Through Movement: Building the Foundation," is a nationally known and highly respected educator-author. She bases her writing on her ongoing work with students of all ages—preschoolers to senior citizens. Her other titles include *Teaching Movement & Dance* and *Round the Circle.*

Phyllis S. Weikart is Associate Professor Emeritus in the Division of Kinesiology, University of Michigan, and visiting Associate Professor at Hartt School of Music. Her formal education includes a B.S. degree from Arcadia University and an M.A. degree from the University of Michigan. In addition to being an educator and author of seven books, she is a researcher, curriculum developer, workshop leader, choreographer, and a producer of high-quality international folk dance albums (with 14 released albums). Her wide-ranging experiences have led to the development of a teaching approach that ensures teachers success with students of all ages.

Related High/Scope® Resources

85 Engaging Movement Activities—Learning on the Move, K–6 Series

The activities in this book will keep your K–6 students jogging, hopping, swaying, rocking, marching, patting, making pathways, and moving in all kinds of ways as they learn. Classroom teachers, as well as specialty teachers in physical education, music, and recreation, will find this book to be a rich source of ideas for challenging and enjoyable movement experiences. The experiences are planned around key curriculum concepts in movement and music as well as in academic curriculum areas such as math and reading. And because these experiences develop students' basic timing, language abilities, vocabulary, concentration, planning skills, and capabilities for cooperative decision making and leadership, teachers will see learning effects that stretch across the curriculum. An easy-to-follow plan is given for each activity: • Suggested level (adaptable for many age groups) • Key experiences in movement and music • Curriculum concepts • Materials needed, including suggested music selections when applicable • Steps for doing each part of the activity • Questions for extending children's understanding • Extension ideas for creative variations. This lively text is enhanced by many illustrations and photos. The attached music CD contains recordings that may be used with many of the activities from this book.

BK-E3040 $34.95

P. S. Weikart and E. B. Carlton. 216 pages, soft cover, illustrated, includes free music CD. 1-57379-125-3

Movement Plus Music: Activities for Children Ages 3 to 7, 2ⁿᵈ Ed.

Outlines movement activities for young children. Focuses on moving in coordinated ways, following directions, feeling and expressing the beat, and moving creatively. Updates many activities and suggests music from the *Rhythmically Moving 1–4* recordings.

BK-M1005 $10.95

P. S. Weikart. Soft cover, 40 pages. 0-931114-96-9

Round the Circle: Key Experiences in Movement for Young Children, 2ⁿᵈ Ed.

Young children learn through play, and their play is full of movement experiences. *Round the Circle* has been completely revised to present the *High/Scope Education Through Movement: Building the Foundation* program for preschoolers developed by Phyllis S. Weikart. This new edition presents *eight key experiences in movement* that help adults *engage, enable,* and *extend* children's active movement explorations. In addition, Weikart's teaching model provides a strong framework for encouraging and supporting young children's learning. Readers will appreciate the numerous *suggested activities, concrete guidelines,* and *effective teaching strategies* that are peppered throughout the book. Use this well-illustrated and easy-to-understand book to make the most of children's movement adventures!

BK-M1020 $24.95

P. S. Weikart. Soft cover, 176 pages. 1-57379-096-6

Movement Plus Rhymes, Songs, & Singing Games, 2ⁿᵈ Ed.

A revised collection of engaging movement activities for children. These activities supplement those described in *Round the Circle* and provide age-appropriate movement experiences. Use them during large-group time, small-group time, or transitions.

BK-M1013 $14.95

P. S. Weikart. Soft cover, 100 pages. 1-57379-066-4

Teaching Movement & Dance: A Sequential Approach to Rhythmic Movement, 5ᵗʰ Ed.

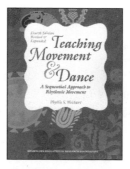

Newly revised, this fifth edition includes updated information on Phyllis S. Weikart's teaching model for beginners of all ages. Also contains over 100 beginning-level dances and instructions for introducing movement and dance in understandable and enjoyable ways. Music for the dances is recorded on the *Rhythmically Moving 1–9* recordings.

BK-M1022 $34.95

P. S. Weikart. Soft cover, 450 pages. 1-57379-132-6

Related High/Scope® Resources

Rhythmically Moving 1–9

Music for students of all ages. Includes suggestions for use with *Teaching Movement & Dance: A Sequential Approach to Rhythmic Movement.* Can also be used with the *Beginning Folk Dances Illustrated* video series and all other folk dance books from High/Scope® Press. Select one or all of these recordings. There is no special order or level of difficulty. Visit our Web site for a complete song list.

P. S. Weikart, creative director. CDs.

Rhythmically Moving 1
BK-M2201 $15.95
0-929816-13-7

Rhythmically Moving 2
BK-M2202 $15.95
0-929816-14-5

Rhythmically Moving 3
BK-M2203 $15.95
0-929816-15-3

Rhythmically Moving 4
BK-M2204 $15.95
0-929816-16-1

Rhythmically Moving 5
BK-M2205 $15.95
0-929816-29-3

Rhythmically Moving 6
BK-M2206 $15.95
0-929816-30-7

Rhythmically Moving 7
BK-M2207 $15.95
0-929816-31-5

Rhythmically Moving 8
BK-M2208 $15.95
0-929816-32-3

Rhythmically Moving 9
BK-M2209 $15.95
0-929816-33-1

Educating Young Children: Active Learning Practices for Preschool and Child Care Programs (2ⁿᵈ Ed.)

The updated chapters include information on phonemic awareness and preschool reading, additional references, the latest Perry Preschool research results, recent research relating to brain development, and a complete description of a consistent approach to problem solving. Written for early childhood practitioners and students, this manual presents essential strategies adults can use to make active learning a reality in their programs. Describes key components of the adult's role: planning the physical setting and establishing a consistent daily routine; creating a positive social climate; and using High/Scopes 58 "key experiences" in child development to understand and support young children. Other topics include family involvement, daily team planning, interest areas, appropriate materials, the plan-do-review process, small- and large-group times. Offers numerous anecdotes, photographs, illustrations, real-life scenarios, and practical suggestions for adults. Reflects High/Scope's current research findings and over 30 years of experience.

BK-P1178 $42.95

M. Hohmann & D. P. Weikart. Soft cover, Lavishly illustrated, 560 pages. 1-57379-104-0

Study Guide to Educating Young Children: Exercises for Adult Learners (2ⁿᵈ Ed.)

This updated workbook will increase your competence and confidence in using the High/Scope Preschool Curriculum. Designed for early childhood college courses, inservice training, and independent study.

Contains exercises that track the content of High/Scope's preschool manual, *Educating Young Children.* Abundant, interactive exercises include hands-on exploration of materials, child studies, analysis of photos and scenarios in *Educating Young Children,* recollection and reflection about curriculum topics, trying out various support strategies, and making implementation plans.

BK-P1179 $17.95

M. Hohmann. Soft cover, 275 pages. 1-57379-163-6

Related High/Scope® Resources

Supporting Young Artists—The Development of the Visual Arts in Young Children

Young children love all kinds of art, and this new book will help you make the most of these natural learning opportunities! It highlights the underlying principles derived from theory, research, and practice and presents the developmental stages in early art-based learning. The authors—both experienced artists and educators—also offer lots of practical information. Learn how to provide appropriate space and materials, plan art-based experiences, and use the language of art to engage with children in a supportive way. Covers drawing and painting, found and recycled materials, paper, and the plastic arts (dough and clay) from the perspectives of enrichment, production, and reflection. An essential handbook for early childhood practitioners in classrooms, centers, and homes as well as university students and professors.

BK-P1192 $34.95

A. S. Epstein & E. Trimis. Soft cover, photos, 288 pages. 1-57379-171-7

Getting Started: Materials and Equipment for Active Learning Preschools

Provides detailed information on selecting materials and equipment for preschools and child care centers. Interest areas covered: art, block, house, toy, book, computer, music and movement, sand and water, woodworking, and outdoor. Includes sample diagrams of typical High/Scope® classrooms and lists of suggested materials, with quantities specified.

BK-P1116 $14.95

N. Vogel. Soft cover, 56 pages. 1-57379-055-9

You Can't Come to My Birthday Party! Conflict Resolution With Young Children

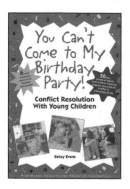

Children's conflicts over toys, space, and friendship create many challenges for teachers and parents. This book presents a six-step mediation process adults can use to support young children at these tense and emotional times. It includes more than 50 actual stories of conflict experiences from preschools, nursery schools, Head Start centers, elementary schools, and homes. Through these stories and the accompanying photos of conflict resolution in action, readers can "see and hear" real children resolving disputes successfully, guided by adults using the six-step process. Using this book as a guide, teachers and parents will have the strategies in hand to make the most of these valuable learning opportunities, whether the children they are caring for are toddlers, preschoolers, or school-aged children.

BK-P1171 $34.95

B. Evans, soft cover, photos, 432 pages. 1-57379-159-8.

Fee, Fie, Phonemic Awareness 130—Prereading Activities for Preschoolers

Endorsed by the High/Scope Early Childhood Reading Institute, this book focuses on phonemic awareness—the ability to recognize the smallest sound units that make up words—identified by reading experts as an essential skill that prepares children for reading. The 130 phonemic awareness activities included in the book are suitable for small-group learning in preschools, prekindergarten programs, Head Start programs, child care centers, and home-based programs. The activities are based on the latest scientific evidence about what children need to become confident and successful readers and writers. They also reflect the research-based, classroom-tested, and internationally recognized teaching strategies of the High/Scope early childhood approach. These brief, self-explanatory, and enjoyable activities require no special teacher training or materials beyond those usually available in active learning early childhood settings. The activities fall into five content categories: identifying sounds, building rhyme awareness, building alliteration awareness, recognizing letters, and developing letter-sound awareness. **The book offers more than enough activities to meet the standard of 20 hours of phonemic awareness practice recommended for all preschool children by the National Reading Panel and endorsed by the U. S. Department of Education.** Also included are a handy chart that helps teachers keep track of the activities experienced and items for assessing children's early reading development using the High/Scope Child Observation Record (COR) for Ages 2½–6.

EE-P1190 $25.95

M. Hohmann. Soft cover, 80 pages, photos. 1-57379-128-8
